# OVERCOMING *TORMENTS OF FEAR*

***Biblical Principles for Deliverance from Fear.***

JAMES WAWERU MWAURA

Utopia Solutions.
P.O. BOX 7204-20100
Nakuru, Kenya.
Tel. 0728071398
michael.ndungu@yahoo.com



P.O. BOX 32818-0100
Nairobi, Kenya
Tel. 0722705470
waweru.james@yahoo.com



All scripture references are taken from New King James Version unless otherwise indicated.

Published by
Utopia Solutions.

ISBN 9798838155054

# Contents

## ACKNOWLEDGMENTS.

First of all, I am forever grateful to God for all His goodness and mercy throughout my life. I thank Him for the priceless and timeless gift of salvation. Restoring fellowship with my Heavenly Father set me on my divine path to my redemptive destiny, gave my life meaning, and guaranteed a life of victory over sin, secularism, and Satan. Everything I am, everything I have, and everything I've done I owe to him. All glory be to God.

Special thanks to my dear wife, Pastor Mary Wanja. You have been a strong pillar of my life, socially, economically, spiritually, and in ministry. I am grateful to you for the blessing and privilege of raising our children with you. Thank you to all my children: Rebecca, Joseph, Peter, Susan, Eunice, Joel, Michael, Mercy, Jane, Veronica, and Ruth for their love, support, and prayers

I sincerely acknowledge my spiritual leaders and mentors: the late Apostle Harry Das, his wife Minister Cora Das, his son John Das and his family. Through their apostolic and prophetic grace, prayers, impartation, teaching, equipping, and training over the past 45 years I have grown and developed into a mature Christian and able minister. I also thank the entire Chrisco family for the love, fellowship, and ministry we have enjoyed together.

My special thanks go to Michael Ndungu and Jane Cosmus, who worked tirelessly to ensure the completion of this book. From creating content to proofreading, and editing, you made the publication of this book a resounding success. I appreciate Jimmy (grandson) for his assistance at the preliminary stage. I'm truly grateful to Pastor Francis K. for your professional input

## Dedication

I dedicate this book to individuals, families, Churches, and Institutions Globally.

May Application of Principles Highlighted in this book bring You Total Freedom from the Tyranny, Torture, confinement and Paralysis of Fear.

## PREFACE

The subject of fear is fascinating and I have taken the time to observe it in my own life and that of people I have ministered to in my 45 years of ministry as a pastor in Christ-Co-Workers Fellowship (Chrisco). I have witnessed how torturous and tyrannical fear can be; it can completely hamper productivity in people's lives if left unchecked. Basically, everyone has their fears, but what one fears differs in both type and magnitude. Although fear has a positive aspect that helps us avoid danger, depending on its severity, it can also be harmful if not managed appropriately. Fear when left unexamined can easily take root and derail your life. Paralyzing Fear must be overcome.

The subject of fear has been widely studied in both the Christian and secular worlds. Christian authors have written to encourage people on how to cope based on biblical principles, while in the secular world coping mechanisms rely on scientific theories and techniques. Psychologists have studied fear and have come up with different classifications and types of fear and how to manage it. My emphasis and primary focus will be the biblical perspective on fear, biblical examples of people who have faced and dealt with different types of fear, and lessons we can learn and apply.

In a review of Genesis Gen 1; 27-28, God created Man and Woman in His image. He blessed them and commanded them to be fruitful, multiply and subdue the earth. Subduing means to bring under control by force or to rule. Man was to rule over the fish, birds in the air, and every creation. This clearly indicates that God never intended us to live in fear, but in dominion, subjecting everything.

The antonyms of fear are courage and boldness emanating from faith and trust in God who is in control of the universe and all human affairs. Whenever God commands His people not to fear, he often calls them to shift their confidence from themselves and their ability to deal with their prevailing situations and to allow God to do it on their behalf, in His way, and by the power of His might.

As Christian believers, we are often confronted with various circumstances that create actual or perceived fear. We need to learn from the

Holy Scriptures to shift our focus from our ability to deal with situations and look to God, the author and finisher of our faith (Hebrews 12:2). Fear not, therefore, for God did not give us the spirit of fear or timidity, but of power and love and a sound mind (2 Timothy 1: 7). We say with confidence; ***"The Lord is my helper, I will not be afraid. What can man do to me***?" (Hebrews 13:6, 8).

I am writing to encourage everyone and the body of Christ to face and overcome their fears. Case studies with biblical and real-life examples will enable you to experience the crippling effects of fear and the principles of dealing with and overcoming different types of fear. All kinds of fears may not be addressed in this book, but believe me, the antidote to all fears is Faith in God.

NOTES

# CHAPTER 1

# UNDERSTANDING THE ORIGIN OF FEAR AND THE TRICHOTOMY OF MAN

## The Ideal Man

In the creation account in Gen 1:27-28, God created man (male and female) in his own image and likeness and breathed the breath of life into his nostrils. He placed him in the Garden of Eden and gave them dominion over all creation.

In Psalm 139 we see the psalmist portraying how God created Man fearfully and wonderfully in his mother's womb, and having great and precious thoughts on him. We also Read in Psalm 8 that man was created a little lower than Angels. God valued man and therefore commanded him to exercise dominion over his creation, be fruitful, multiply, fill the earth and subdue it.

In his original state (Pre-fall state), the man was meant to be a reflection of God's nature and attributes. Consequently, man lived in harmony with God, himself, others, and his environment. This is evident from the peaceful coexistence between man and wild beast, and with God. We see God often visiting them in the Garden of Eden to fellowship with them daily in the cool of the day (Gen 2:1).

## The Fall and Redemption of Man.

However, this harmony was disrupted and destroyed by man's disobedience as recorded in Gen 3:1-7. The devil deceived man and he ate the fruit of the forbidden tree in the middle of the garden which was of the knowledge of good and evil.

The immediate reaction was that man realized he was naked and he was **AFRAID** of God and hid from Him (Gen 1:8-10). This was the first **(origin)** emotional expression of FEAR in the History of mankind. Consequently, man forfeited the abundant life that God intended for him, and enmity ensued between man, wild beasts, and his environment. Its apparent from this account Fear was a by-product of sin, the strongest weapon of the devil, it deprives man of his original destiny, alienates him from God, and interferes with relationships (Genesis 3:15).

Man in his fallen nature could no longer function in the completeness and perfection that God created him. God originally created him in his own image and likeness, but this was corrupted by sin. Because of the corruption of sin, man could no longer act in and reflect his divine character. Evil and ungodly thoughts and feelings began to emanate from the fallen man's heart.

All negative emotions such as fear, jealousy, envy, bitterness, pride, sadness, and anger not only sprang from the heart of the fallen man but also began to control man. These negative emotions are a natural reaction to unpleasant situations and are meant to help us adapt better to our ecosystem, but when they control us and lead to negative behavior, we become unproductive and need help.

For example, immediately after the fall, we see Cain killing his brother Abel. He was overcome with jealousy and anger when God graciously accepted Abel's sacrifice and rejected his offering (Gen. 4:3-8). We also witness fear dominating God's people like Abraham, Isaac, the children of Israel, and others.

When Abraham went to Egypt, he feared that the men of the city would kill him because of Sarah's beauty and take her away from him. To save his life, he lies that she was his sister. Sarah was kidnapped by Abimelech the king, but God intervened, rebuked him, and commanded him to return her to Abraham (Genesis 12:7-10).

The same scenario was repeated in the life of his son Isaac (Gen. 26:7-10). In Exodus 14:10-13 we read the story of the children of Israel on their departure from Egypt. After Pharaoh freed them, they found themselves on the shore of the Red Sea. The pharaoh repented for releasing them and immediately mobilized and deployed his army to pursue them. When the Israelites saw them being pursued, they began to wail and complain out of fear. They wished they had died in Egypt rather than in the wilderness.

The theme of fear runs throughout Scripture. We also see God encouraging His people not to fear because he would protect them and deliver them from their enemies. The statement: **"Do not be Afraid"** occurs very frequently in the Bible. Fear is by no means God's nature, as He does not give us the spirit of fear, but sound a mind (2 Timothy 1:7). This implies that fear is of our enemy, the devil. We must overcome it and not let it control our lives.

Man in his fallen state could no longer be like God in his nature unless God redeems him and restores him to the place of dominion. God has always pursued man since the fall through righteous men and prophets and eventually sent his only Son Jesus Christ to pay the price of man's ransom once and for all (Hebrews 7:27).

By believing in the finished work of the cross we become children of God (John 1:1-3). As children of God, we are entitled and empowered to recover everything we have lost through sin.

## The Tripartite Man

God created Man as a tripartite being meaning that he is made up of three components namely; spirit, soul, and body (1 Thessalonians 5:23). The body interacts with the physical realm through the five senses namely, sight, smell, hearing, touch, and taste.

The soul consists of our invisible being where thoughts and emotions stem from. It's the area where psychologists major on. Spirit is also our inner being that connects with the spiritual realm. It allows us to experience and connects with spiritual matters.

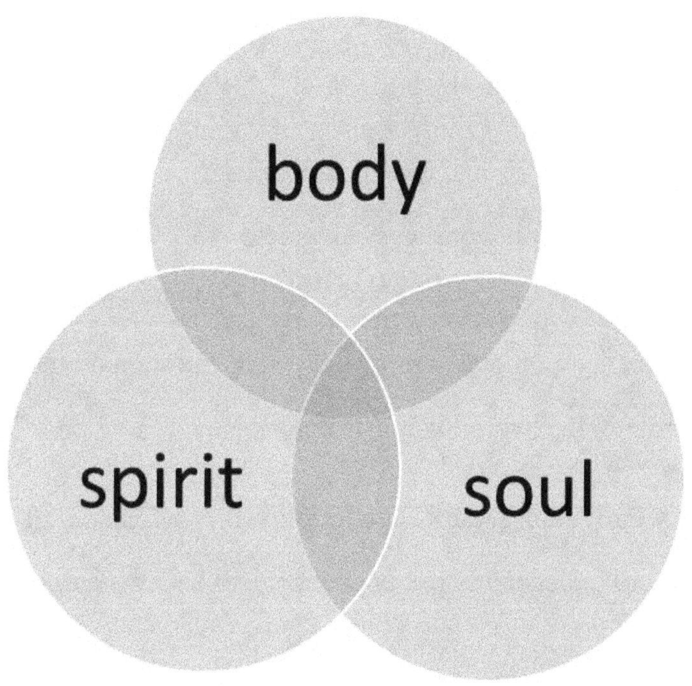


**Relationship between the three components of Man**

The three components do not exist independently of each other but rather mutually interact and affect each other. For example, what one sees in the physical realm can affect how one feels and reacts (soul). What

**Every individual should have Emotional Intelligence (EI), which is the ability to understand, use, and manage one's own emotions in positive ways to reduce stress, communicate effectively, empathize with others, overcome challenges, and defuse conflict**

you feel can also be influenced by your beliefs (spiritual).

## Understanding the Emotions of Man

As I explained above, the human being is a three-part being and the three components constantly interact. While many are aware of and take care of their physical body, not many pay attention to their emotional being and take care of it as well. Emotional well-being plays a key role in the overall welfare of a person.

Every individual should have Emotional Intelligence (EI), which is the ability to understand, use, and manage one's own emotions in positive ways to reduce stress, communicate effectively, empathize with others, overcome challenges, and defuse conflict

Emotions play an adaptive role in human beings, as emphasized in the preface. Psychologists and researchers have taken the time to study emotions extensively and have developed various theories to explain how emotions help people adapt to their ecosystem.

## Classification of Emotions

Emotions are classified according to how far they can be distinguished from one another. Pleasant emotions accompany the successful attainment of our intended goals, while unpleasant emotions accompany frustrated efforts to achieve specific intended goals in life. Emotions vary in these different ways:

Emotions vary in the following ways.

a) Intensity: mild, moderate, or severe

b) Range: range from positive to negative

c) Purity: emotions are either pure or a blend of more than one emotion. For example, primary emotion is like grief and ecstasy, and those that are blended like jealousy which is a blend of love + fear.

d) They also exist in opposites: love vs. hatred, joy vs sadness.

## Components of Emotions.

From a psychological perspective, every emotion has:

i. A particular affect or feeling can be labeled as love, joy, fear, etc.
ii. Physiological arousal: which represents bodily changes mediated by the limbic system that prepares the individual to handle the crisis that is fight or flight. This may include an increase in heartbeat, sweat and increased breathing, etc.
iii. A cognitive state: involves interpretation of the situation i.e. whether to fight or take flight.
iv. Behavioral reactions i.e. overt expression of the emotions. Generally, emotions can act as motivations for our behavior. We can act or avoid certain circumstances due to the expected consequences real or perceived.

## Relationship between Emotions and Motivation.

Emotions can acts as a motivation for our behavior especially when we anticipate pleasant feelings. Emotions also serve as a signal to tell us what to do and what to avoid. Emotions also accompany our actions.

This understanding helps us see how fear, which is an emotion, can affect our actions (physically) and also how our beliefs (spiritually) can affect our feelings and then our actions. It's important to note that our feelings play a key role in determining our behavior, which subsequently becomes our way of life (lifestyle).

Psychologists have discovered that people maintain behaviors that bring them consistent pleasure while avoiding those that make them uncomfortable. This means that a behavior is likely to be repeated as long as it makes us feel comfortable. In general, this means that emotions can be the foundation of our behavior.

Therefore, based on the above understanding, we see that fear can serve as the basis for certain behaviors designed to avoid harm/danger. While these aspects are good for keeping us from danger, these fears may be based on irrational thoughts and beliefs about the objects or animals, or circumstances rather than reality. These distorted thoughts can lead to irrational fears that can affect our productivity in life.

Psychologists call these fears phobias, which can be categorized into fear of heights, fear of large bodies of water, fear of darkness, fear of open space, fear of certain insects, fear of animals, and fear of certain situations.

If the fear is not tamed, it can develop into phobias that can easily trigger panic attacks. Symptoms of panic attacks include extreme anxiety, and physical sensations such as increased heart rate, shortness of breath, tremors, and muscle tension.

This book addresses various situational fears by highlighting just a few examples and showing how to deal with them based on biblical principles

NOTES

# Chapter 2.

# TRAGEDY OF FEAR: WHAT YOU FEAR WILL HAPPEN.

The story of Job is very popular and well known to many. A brief examination of his life will reveal the devastation of fear in his life.

## Accurate introduction of Job and Epic commendation from God.

The book of Job begins with a precise introduction and a magnificent classical praise o Job by God.

Job 1:1-5, ***"There was a man in the land of Uz whose name was Job, and that man was blameless and upright, one who feared God and turned away from evil. There were born to him seven sons and three daughters. He possessed 7,000 sheep, 3,000 camels, 500 yokes of oxen, and 500 female donkeys, and very many servants so that this man was the greatest of all the people of the east. His sons used to go***

***and hold a feast in the house of each one on his day, and they would send and invite their three sisters to eat and drink with them. And when the days of the feast had run their course, Job would send and consecrate them, and he would rise early in the morning and offer burnt offerings according to the number of them all. For Job said, "It may be that my children have sinned, and cursed God in their hearts." Thus Job did continually."(***ESV)

## The Tragedy of Job.

After, the introduction and commendation, we are treated with an interjection. The scene suddenly shifts from the Earth to Heaven. There is a meeting of the sons of God (Angels) and surprisingly Satan also appears. God turns His attention to him and Job features as the subject of their discussion. The conclusion of their discussion was God permitted Satan to test Job (Job 1:6-12).

Job 1:13-22, "***Now there was a day when his sons and daughters were eating and drinking wine in their oldest brother's house, and there came a messenger to Job and said, "The oxen were plowing and the donkeys feeding beside them, and the Sabeans fell upon them and***

***took them and struck down the servants with the edge of the sword, and I alone have escaped to tell you." While he was yet speaking, there came another and said, "The fire of God fell from heaven and burned up the sheep and the servants and consumed them, and I alone have escaped to tell you." While he was yet speaking, there came another and said, "The Chaldeans formed three groups and made a raid on the camels and took them and struck down the servants with the edge of the sword, and I alone have escaped to tell you.***

***" While he was yet speaking, there came another and said, "Your sons and daughters were eating and drinking wine in their oldest brother's house, and behold, a great wind came across the wilderness and struck the four corners of the house, and it fell upon the young people, and they are dead, and I alone have escaped to tell you."***

***Then Job arose and tore his robe and shaved his head and fell on the ground and worshiped. And he said, "Naked I came from my mother›s womb, and naked shall I return. The Lord gave, and the Lord has taken away; blessed be the name of the Lord."***

***In all this Job did not sin or charge God with wrong."***

## What You Fear will Happen.

After hearing the sad news and seeing the evidence of his great loss, Job broke down so offended, confused, and filled with pain and anger; like most of us would have done or worse.

But here's the secret we all need to learn. The Bible says that Job sat for days with his clothes torn (sackcloth) and in pain (symbolizing deep pain and regret). He didn't speak or eat for seven good days. The next thing that came out of his mouth were these few words

***"The thing I feared the most has come upon me, and that which I was afraid of has come unto me."*** (Job 3:25).

This statement is not only perplexing but reveals the underlying and controlling traits of fear in Job's heart. Although he was a godly man and avoided evil, he had faults; little fears in the closet of his heart. The Bible speaks of how he always went out to make atonement for his children whenever they were feasting and rejoicing.

While there may not seem to be anything wrong with a parent getting up early in the morning and pleading with the Lord for their children, the problem is one of motivation. Job made these daily sacrifices for each child because he was **AFRAID** that something bad would happen to them if he didn't. While the ritual and routine seemed harmless enough, it was not performed in faith. Job did this out of **fear** and we all know what happened to his children. Later, as our focus text shows, Job said, **what I always feared happened to me. What I feared has come true.**

It was his everyday fear that he might lose everything he had earned over the years. His cattle, mansions, cars, ranch, businesses, family, everything (whatever you call it) and come back to a zero point. He moved through his daily tasks with these fears embedded deep within his being

I'm pretty sure he would spend hours imagining what it would feel like to lose everything and the pain he must go through trying to gain it all back. I would like to believe that it was on one of those many days, as he sat relaxed in his comfortable chair in his beautifully landscaped garden when he heard the sad news of the loss of his children, cattle, farmland, mansions, and even his servants.

He lost everything he had ever worked for around the same time.

Most believers know the story of Job, but most don't know that Job allowed fear to open the door to some of the horrible things that happened in his life. Just as your godly Faith opens the door for the things of God in your life, your fear opens the door for the things of the enemy. In many ways, fear is just like Faith, but in a negative form.

**Most believers know the story of Job, but most don't know that Job allowed fear to open the door to some of the horrible things that happened in his life. Just as your godly Faith opens the door for the things of God in your life, your fear opens the door for the things of the enemy. In many ways, fear is just like Faith, but in a negative form. The more afraid you are of something, the more vulnerable you are to it.**

The more afraid you are of something, the more vulnerable you are to it. So if you get up early every morning and pray for your children, marriage, health, career, finances, relationships, Nation, etc., but do it out of fear, then your prayers will have no effect.

We are to pray in faith, not in fear. Not only does fear-based prayer have no power, but even worse, when you are afraid, you literally open the door for what you fear to come upon you. What does that mean for you today? It means you can stop the cycle of fear in your life. This revelation is designed to uncover the enemy's plans so you can live a victorious life in Christ and experience a powerful and effective prayer life. The antidote to fear is faith, let all your spiritual activities be motivated by faith and not fear.

## When what You Fear Happens.

God knows us so well and Satan knows us too. Our weaknesses; things we fear can be used to test our faith in God. We should maintain our integrity even amid trials. Job never cursed God or accused him of any wrongdoing.

Never lose your faith in God. His word says he will provide a way of escape (1 Corinthians 10:13). As you read this book, you may be going through these very difficult moments in your life, but there is one thing to remember: He says he will never leave us or let us down (Hebrews 13:5, Isaiah 49:6). Overcome the tendency to give up, keep praying, and just as Job did, you will come out victorious, stronger, and better.

NOTES

# Chapter 3

# FEAR TORMENTS: MY FEAR EXPERIENCES.

## 1. Fear of Road Accident.

Back in September 1976 while working at the Treasury House in the ministry of Finance in the accounts department. I constantly used public service vehicles to commute to and from my rented abode in Nairobi and also on monthly basis to Nyandarua which is my remote county of residence.

All was well until the year 1980 when my father fell ill and this necessitated traveling home more frequently to see how he was fairing. On one of those trips, I started being afraid of being involved in a road accident as I traveled home. The fear was growing stronger every other trip.

One weekend, as I was preparing to travel home, the fear was so intense "Do I go home or do I postpone?" but considering the state of my father, I still had to travel home. When I arrived home, the state of my dad necessitated him to be taken to hospital. On the morning of the following day, I had to take my father to the hospital in Nakuru with a plan of travelling to Nairobi the same day. I took my father to the hospital but fear was becoming stronger and louder, I resolved not to travel but rather go back home.

I hoped that the fear would go as I spent the night at home, unfortunately, during the night I had a very vivid dream of being involved in a road accident on my way back to Nairobi and this intensified my fear even more. When I woke up, I was so much afraid and my dilemma was "If I travel to Nairobi, the dream was very clear I will be involved in an accident, if I don't travel to Nairobi, the consequences are quite clear, I will lose my treasured job at the Treasury. I will also lose my personal belongings in Nairobi." After Much prayers and contemplation, I resolved to travel to Nairobi.

I started extended prayers after which I gained some courage to start my Journey to Nairobi. When I boarded the vehicle headed to Nairobi I started reading the word of God to encourage myself in the Lord as I waited for the car to be full. The dreaded journey started, and I reasoned within myself "It would be more traumatizing to experience the accident consciously" So I decided to doze off. As fate would have it, my sleep was interrupted At Naivasha when the vehicle I was traveling in was stopped by traffic police for a brief inspection.

The inspection didn't take long and the journey continued but I couldn't doze again. We continued with the journey smoothly until when we reached Muguga near Sigona golf club. "In the twinkling of an eye, I saw An over speeding bus headed to Nakuru attempting to overtake multiple vehicles and now was headed for a head-on collision with our vehicle, In my mind, I had no shadow of a doubt, what I feared and dreamt about is inevitably happening as I helplessly watched. As a Christian believer, I was instantly quickened and called out aloud "JESUS! Jesus! Jesus!"

I knew everyone that calls on the name of Jesus shall be saved. Acts 2:21 for He can send his angels to rescue us from the situation lest we dash against a stone as stated in Psalm 91:11-12. It was at that moment that our driver realized that we were headed for would be a

Serious head-on collision, instinctively He swerved out of the road avoiding head-on collision by a whisker, but unfortunately, the vehicle overturned upside down.

The vehicle was designed in such a way that the passengers would sit in one open space facing one another thus they were pushed from one side to another downwards hitting each other. Many of the passengers were injured by the metallic seats and the floor of the overturned vehicle. One passenger who had slept throughout the journey was pronounced dead on arrival at Kikuyu hospital, while several other passengers sustained varying degrees of injuries.

In my case, the dream at night and the feelings of intense fear prompted me to pray more intensely concerning the situation and I can only describe this narrow escape as a miraculous deliverance and protection by God as a result of prayer. Although I was seated in the driver's cabin with the driver and another young man.

When I proclaimed the name Jesus three times, he released his angel to tie me with invisible safety belts. The driver was the first to be thrown out of the vehicle followed by the young man after the vehicle overturned but to my surprise, although I was seated in the middle seat and now facing downwards, I was not falling off. Miraculous safety belts were holding me up so I had to sit up and sneak out of the vehicle without having even a single bruise. God used this involvement in an accident to demonstrate his mighty deliverance and help me overcome the fear of accidents from there on.

God sent his angels who are ministering spirits to the heirs of salvation. (Hebrews 1: 14). He sends them to rescue, to deliver a message, or to warn people of their wrongdoing. On realizing that the only passenger who died was asleep throughout the journey, I concluded that God had used the traffic police in Naivasha to wake me up so that I can call on the name of Jesus for the salvation of many, I included. After treatment of Passengers with minor injuries and recording statements at the police station, we were later allowed to travel by another bus

From that incident onwards, I did not fear traveling by public means for a period of another ten more years until the Lord gave me my vehicle in 1990. This miraculous deliverance was such an encounter with God's power that prepared me for life.

I continued working for ten more years when I opted to take early retirement from civil service into full-time ministry having worked for 18 years.

## 2. Fear that has cost Me an amputated Leg

Fear more often than not is based on irrational thoughts and it can be so controlling that it affects us negatively. From a young age, I had a rare kind of irrational fear of hospital admission, injection, and drugs and I didn't want any visit to the Hospital. This did not necessarily mean that I didn't fall sick and needed to use drugs but more often than not, I would just buy over-the-counter drugs and sometimes not even finish the prescribed dose.

I remember a certain incident in my younger life while still working as a civil servant when I developed fever and tonsils and I had to go to the hospital. I pleaded with the doctor not to inject me but rather to give me the medications and he gave in after going home I didn't take the drugs as prescribed and this necessitated a second visit to the hospital and now I couldn't escape an injection as before.

Sometimes back in 2016, I was pierced by a rusted nail and I didn't go to the hospital for the tetanus injection because of fear of injection and medication. What I didn't know is that the infection that was caused by the nail kept worsening and spreading through the leg.

There were frequent episodes of severe pains that acted as warning signs but the fear of going to the hospital and getting injected couldn't allow me to go for a checkup. For a period of five 5 years, I superficially dressed the wound with salty water and chloride antiseptic but this only suppressed the pains temporarily.

The wound would later recur in a more severe condition and as usual, self-dress it at home.

However, In June 2021, the wound became stinky and pussy. On 12th June 2021, I started feeling dizzy, weakling, and unable to stand on my own. For two days I was confined to bed wishing that the sickening feelings will fade away.

With the situation getting out of hand, going to Hospital was inevitable. I, therefore, was rushed to the hospital in Nakuru on 14th June 2021. On that particular day, my blood sugar level had spiked to 34 points glucometer. The sugar levels were stabilized but the wound still needed specialized medical attention necessitating my referral to AIC Kijabe Hospital. Initial Examination at AIC Kijabe hospital started revealing the seriousness of wound infection and the confirmed diabetes had severely affected my right foot calling for an emergency Debridement surgery.

I was booked for minor debridement surgery. Unfortunately, when I was taken to the theatre, the surgeon realized that the effect on my foot was more severe than they had initially thought. To my shock, I was informed that the only solution to treat my condition, was to amputate my right foot below the knee.

I vehemently resisted but after seeking for second medical opinion and consultation with family members and much counseling, I consented to the inevitable amputation surgery. This reality of losing part of my leg in my seventies whereas all along, I enjoyed rather a good health without a visit to the hospital was not easy.

At this point now, I not only got injections and drugs but was also admitted for one week for observation. This irrational fear has not only cost me part of my leg, but also a lot of time as I nurse my wound. My productivity and efficiency in different things I enjoyed before like visits to my gardens and seeing my livestock have significantly been reduced during this period.

I may not reverse the effects of fear but what I can for sure say is that fear is not of God but of our foe whose work is to steal kill and destroy John 10:10b. This has taught me a lot that fear should always be faced and overcome in Faith. This experience has served as an agent of deliverance from the fear of hospital experience.

I believe that God is interested in us living fulfilled lives away from all kinds of fear and sometimes he may allow us to go through the experiences we fear so that he can build our faith and purge us from that sin that holds us captive. As I live the rest of the years that God gives me, I will seek to glorify him more in every circumstance and will not allow the enemy to oppress me again with any form of fear.

May God help you also as you read through these experiences to allow God to purge you of every fear so that you not only live a more fulfilled life but also be productive in every way for His glory.

## 3. Fear of Court Cases.

The word of God exhorts us to live in harmony with one another and to seek peace with all men as long as we can Rom 12:17, 18. I cherish peace and harmony as long as I can seek and promote them. He also exhorts us to settle matters quickly with our adversary before we are handed over to the judge and the judge puts us in prison Matt 5:25.

In my endeavors to seek peaceful coexistence, sometimes it's not easy because not everyone seeks to be peaceful. Conflicts may arise from situations we less expect and sometimes we are not able to solve them amicably since some people are selfish and want to be unjust in any situation thus the court must be involved.

Since I know the rigorous process of the courts in terms of money and time spent I feared being involved in a court case. I recall an incident when I was involved in an accident at Delamere Naivasha near Kobil petrol station the accident involved a Government of Kenya (Gk) vehicle a Mercedes Benz and my vehicle.

The Gk vehicle wanted to stop by the roadside but the driver of the

Mercedes Benz couldn't notice the indicator and thus finally hit him from behind and since I was following him I also hit him from behind. The GK towed the Benz to the police station and I also went to write a statement.

The GK left immediately after towing the Benz to the police station and we were both left to write a statement. To my surprise, it looked like they conspired against me since the Benz driver changed the whole story and said that I hit him from behind and he hit a tree. I was enraged but there was no one to testify of what exactly happened.

The case was then filed in court. I waited for the court sessions and I went for the first, second, and third mentioning of the case without the accuser appearing. It was during the third court session I met a lawyer friend who advised me on what to do.

He advised me to inform the court that I had appeared three times in court but the accuser did not appear and it was expensive in terms of time and money. When my name was called out in court, I made my submission as the lawyer had advised me and there was sufficient reason for the case to be terminated.

I celebrated the termination of the case but little did I know that the Mercedes Benz owner was still scheming on how to pursue me. It was after a while that one day some people from an auction firm appeared in my office with a court order to auction office equipment to pay for the towing expenses from Naivasha to Nairobi and the repair of the vehicle which was amounting to one hundred and twenty thousand Kenyan shillings.

I had to pay the expenses since I didn't want to be involved in the court cases again or lose my office equipment. I kept wondering where the court order to auction my properties came from yet the same court had terminated the case!

The whole ordeal was quite distressing but I realized since we live in a broken world there are situations we may never be able to avoid and instead of being fearful we should trust God even as we go through them.

He may sometimes allow us to go through the fearful situation so that we learn to trust him through it all. I have since then forgiven him since I was unjustly made to bear the cost.

Although he didn't deserve it, I forgave him since I have also been forgiven many times by the lord even when I didn't deserve it (Matt18:21-35).

NOTES

# Chapter 4

## OVERCOMING FEAR OF LOSING THE FAMILY INHERITANCE.

Inheritance is bequeathing of the rights to own the deceased estates to the living descendants. The rights are transferable throughout generations.

**Proverbs 13; 22 says, *"A good man leaves an inheritance for their children's children but a sinners wealth is stored up for the righteous".***

**In Genesis 12:1,** God called Abraham and told him to leave his home country and go to the land of Canaan. He promised to give it to him and his descendants as an inheritance.

The issue of inheritance is a Biblical concept that God was interested in from the beginning. It is about the continuity of life and generations and thus an important issue that affects many. More often, the bequeathal process begins upon the death of the person concerned. It involves sharing what the deceased acquired while they were alive, as nobody carries their wealth with them when they die. Job confirms in Job 1:21 that they come naked and return naked.

## Who has the Right to Inherit Family Wealth.

Due to conflicts that arise in the bequeathal process, many countries all over the world have laws that govern the inheritance and bequeathal process. They spell out the age, legitimacy, and gender issues and honor the will of the deceased. This subject is of the utmost importance as it affects posterity.

Family inheritance law regulates who is entitled to the family inheritance and defines the groups of people who are allowed to file applications as follows:

a) The spouse or civil (registered) partner of the deceased;

b) The former spouse or civil partner of the deceased (as long as that person has not remarried/entered into a subsequent civil partnership);

c) A person who, for the two years before the death, was living with the deceased as a spouse or civil partner;

d) A child of the deceased;

e) A person who was treated as a child by the deceased;

f) Any other person who was being maintained by the deceased before their death.

A person is said to have been maintained by the deceased if they were financially supported, directly or indirectly, by the deceased. Nature of maintenance range from gifts given by the deceased during their lifetime, to simply providing an indirect benefit, such as by permitting a person to live rent-free in their home.

## Causes of Conflicts in the sharing of the Family Inheritance.

The issue of bequeathing the inheritance rights is sometimes marred by wrangles and conflicts. Disputes and conflicts emanate from different factors that seek to determine the legitimacy of the heir, age of the heir, and sibling rivalry among many other factors.

Media around the World keeps reporting stories of wrangles and conflicts within families over family inheritance. Although some may seem trivial and silly, the study shows that it is not about triviality and greed. Money and inheritances are symbols with attached meaning and importance. The symbols can represent love, safety, self-esteem, connectedness, and immortality.

They represent the heirs' struggle to feel love and importance. Some studies have shown that there are some basic reasons why families fight in matters of inheritance that may include:

1. The genetic predisposition of all humans to competition and conflict;
2. The psychological sense of self-worth is intertwined with the approval of what an inheritance represents, especially when the deceased is a parent;
3. Genetically, humans are hard-wired to be on the lookout for exclusion, sometimes finding it even when it doesn't exist.
4. Families may also fight because the death of a loved one activates the death anxieties of those left behind.
5. In some cases, one or more members of a family may have a

partial or full-blown personality disorder that causes them to distort and escalate natural family rivalries into personal and legal battles.

6. Dysfunctional families.
7. Some of the heirs or siblings are mentally ill or addicted.

## Dynamics that Exacerbate Family disputes

1. A polygamous family,
2. Divorce Cases where the Court was not involved.
3. Lack of a written will by the deceased person.
4. Lack of knowledge of the legislative aspects of the family inheritance.
5. Corruption; this is where an unjust ruling is made in favor of one party due to a bribe.
6. Lack of resources for a good lawyer to argue the case in court.

## Biblical Accounts on Family Inheritance.

## The Threat of losing Family Inheritance due to Legitimacy issues.

Proverbs 13:22 says a good man leaves the inheritance to his children and their children's children. The inability to bear children is so distressing and often seen as a curse. It threatens the continuity of the surname and even if the family is wealthy, one may see it as pointless to leave it to other people who are not his/her biological children. This was the fate of Abraham, the man we know today as the hero of faith in the Bible.

When God called Him, Abraham was 75 years old while his wife Sarah was 65. They were still childless because Sarah was barren and of advanced age. God promised to give them their son as an heir. Over time, Sarah grew impatient and devised a plan to have children. She gave Abraham her maid to sleep with her.

She conceived and gave birth to a son named Ishmael. In keeping with His promise, God miraculously gave Abraham and Sarah a son when they were a hundred100) and Ninety (90) years respectively (Genesis21:10-13). When Isaac was born Sarah saw Ishmael as a mockery. To disinherit him, Sarah told Abraham to drive out Hagar and her son. Abraham was greatly distressed because it concerned his son. However, God told him to act on what Sarah said because he would be reckoned through Isaac though He promised to make Ishmael a great Nation too. This case of legitimacy is not unique to Isaac and Ismael only.

Many people lose their inheritance due to legitimacy issues. Some are born out of wedlock while others are in a polygamous families. Those from second or third wives might not be considered legitimate children and thus conflicts ensue on whether they should inherit.

## The Threat of losing Family Inheritance due Sibling rivalry and Trickery.

## (Gen27:1-45)

When Isaac became of age, he married Rebecca and they begat twin sons, Esau the firstborn, and Jacob the second born. Jacob was a favorite of his mother Rebecca. Esau was a skillful hunter and his father enjoyed his game meat. In old age, the father wanted to hand over his blessing and inheritance to the firstborn as the custom was. He requested Esau to go to the field, get some game and prepare it for him so that after eating he would bless him. Sometimes back, Jacob had beguiled his brother to sell his birthright to Him.

On that fateful day, Esau had gone hunting in the fields as usual but was quite unlucky. He returned home exhausted, hungry, and in despair. When he got home, he begged Jacob to serve him a morsel of bread and lentil soup. However, Jacob demanded that he sell his birthright in exchange for one plate of food.

Esau did not hesitate to sell his birthright to him. So on the day, Isaac was to bless Esau, he instructed him to hunt and prepare for him delicious game meat he loved so that after eating, he would bless him. Rebecca their mother overheard this conversation and because she preferred Jacob, She quickly prepared a delicious goat stew and gave it to Jacob who cunningly served his father.

After eating, the father blessed Jacob instead of Esau. He, therefore, managed to get the inheritance that was meant for his older brother but not without dire consequences. He had no option but to run away for his life from his enraged brother who wanted to kill him. He found refuge at his uncle Laban's home where he toiled for 20 years. This biblical case is not exceptional since many lose their inheritance in such circumstances of trickery and sibling rivalry. Many have impending court cases while others have regrettably lost their lives in the process.

## The Risk of losing Family Inheritance because of Gender.

The world is generally a Patriarchal society and customary males are regarded and preferred as heirs more than females. Sons are considered the heir because daughters get married and move away to join their husbands and are therefore considered to inherit from their spouses' families.

It's quite a concern when a family has only daughters as was in this case of Zelophehad's daughters recorded in Numbers 27:1-11. They were all born daughters and no law existed at the moment on how to address such situations.

They were on the verge of losing their family inheritance when they decided to seek a determination of the matter from Moses who was the leader and judge of Israel at the time. Moses inquired about the matter with God and He gave him law and instructions to govern inheritance in such scenarios. In case the deceased had no sons, the daughters were permitted to inherit family wealth but had to be married within their clan. This way the family of the deceased would not lose their inheritance and the clan inheritance too would not be forfeited.

The case of Zelophehad's daughters is a societal issue where if a family has only daughters it's a real threat to them losing the entire family wealth. In other families, when their parents die it leads to some families separating, divorcing, or remarrying to get male children.

In Kenya and other countries, legislation has been passed to allow the female gender to inherit the family wealth. If such is your case like Zelophehad's daughters, address it first to the lord and then to the existing law of the land and God will give you a breakthrough.

### The Threat of losing Family Inheritance due to unjust Governing Authority.

The will of the deceased is not to sell family wealth for posterity and to preserve their inheritance. Such is the case recorded in 1 king 21. Naboth had a parcel of land near the king's palace. Out of greed, King Ahab coveted Naboth's land. He requested Naboth to sell it to him or in exchange the king would give him another parcel of land. Naboth however declined all the king's offers. He told off the King on his face that he can't sell his father's inheritance.

the Queen however schemed assassination of Naboth and they grabbed the parcel of land. God was displeased with Ahab and Jezebel and punished his house to avenge Naboth's blood. In event that you are entangled in land or property tussle with senior authorities who abuse their authority to oppress you, always seek help from God.

As you pursue the legal address of your case, Involve God who is the Just Judge. Though you may lose inheritance to cases of injustice, God is the defender of the weak and will always fight and avenge us.

## The Threat losing Family Inheritance due to the Age of the Heir. (Luke 15:11-32).

In the New Testament, we are told of the story of the prodigal son who demanded his inheritance even before the appointed time. Upon receiving his share of the inheritance, he traveled to a faraway country and squandered all his possession with reckless living. Out of desperation, when he came back to his senses, he went back to his father and apologized.

His father graciously pardoned and received him back.

From these biblical examples, we can witness factors that determine and influence the administration of inheritance;

a) The will of the deceased. In the case of Naboth, they were forbidden to sell their inheritance.

b) Gender issue. Zelophehad's daughters were on the verge of losing their family inheritance due to their gender.

c) Legitimacy. The case of Isaac and Ishmael who was expelled.

d) Culture and tradition. In the case of Esau and Jacob, the blessing of the Firstborn was a Jewish culture.

Some of the negative outcomes of sibling and relatives rivalry over family inheritance are witnessed in these accounts:

a) Court cases: Zelophehad's daughters had to seek the legal address of their matter from Moses who was the leader and judge.

b) Murder: Naboth was murdered by Ahab and Jezebel.

c) Prolonged conflicts and rivalry: Esau sought to kill Jacob. Jacob had to run and stay in a kind of exile for 20 years.

d) Family break-ups: Ishmael was expelled from Abraham's home.

In Kenya, there are many court battles regarding inheritance. Some are injured while others die awaiting the determination of their case. To address these challenges, the government enacted laws especially to protect the windows who often time are denied the right to own the estates of their deceased husbands by their in-laws.

### How to face the Fear of losing Family Inheritance.

As Christian, when faced with such challenges, our response should not be fear but rather

1. Understand the laws of your country governing the process of bequeathal. This may require the engagement of government officials or a lawyer.

2. Use the law of the land to defend your case.

3. Ensure you possess the right legal documents: marriage certificate, Title deeds, The identity card, and will of the deceased

4. Seek divine intervention. God is the sovereign and righteous Judge. Present your case to the Lord in prayer. He is the defender of the weak and he can deliver you from all injustices.

5. Understand that we are pilgrims and sojourners in this world. Our **greatest** desire is to inherit the greater eternal riches of the Kingdom of God, which moth and rust cannot destroy (Matt 6:19-20). ***"For what will a man gain if they gain the whole world and lose their own soul"*** **(Matthew 16:26). In the parable of the rich fool, Jesus warned us against hoarding too much earthly wealth and not being rich toward** God(Luke 18:22-25). My prayer we shall seek first the kingdom of God and His righteousness and all these other things will be added as well (Matt. 6:33).

Therefore don't fear and encourage others not to fear because God is in control of all affairs of men.

NOTES

# Chapter 6

## OVERCOMING FEAR OF FAILURE

Fear of failure is also called ***atychiphobia.*** It derives from the Greek words ***"atyches"*** which means unfortunate and ***"Phobia"*** meaning fear.

Atychiphobia is a persistent, excessive, and unrealistic fear of failure that causes you to avoid or put off any activity, scenario, or situation that has the potential of unfortunate or unsuccessful results. This condition prevents someone from taking risks, embracing growth, or trying new things

If you don't meet your goals and expectations, you're not a failure. You become a failure when you allow that fear to hold you back from activities that have the potential to lead you to success. It develops as a result of multiple failures leading to one developing a failure mentality.

It is pragmatically impossible to go through life without some kind of failure. Don't see failure as the end of the world, a proof of your inadequacy, but as an incredible learning experience that will help you grow and avoid making the same mistake again.

Most of the successful people we celebrate today failed at some point in their life. For example, Michael Jordan who is widely considered one of the greatest basketball players of all time was dropped from his high school basketball team because his coach thought he wasn't good enough.

Warren Buffet, one of the world's richest and most successful business gurus was rejected by Harvard University. Richard Branson owner of Virgin Empire is a high school dropout.

You will fail in life, doors will be closed to you and you may make bad decisions, but never let those mistakes and bad decisions define you.

Through failure, we sometimes learn valuable lessons and gain experiences that we otherwise would not have been able to achieve. It can also help you discover trustworthy friends and find new energy for success. Valuable insights are gained from failure.

## Symptoms of Fear of Failure.

A person with atychiphobia may experience one or more of the following symptoms:

1. A reluctance to try new things or engage in challenging tasks. Fear of attempting simple tasks at work, home, or school.
2. Self-Sabotage: Manifested as procrastination, excessive anxiety when trying to do something or failure to achieve goals. High distractibility, being distracted by irrelevant or unimportant things
3. Low self-esteem or self-confidence: The feelings of inadequacy are often expressed through negative statements such as I'm not good enough, I'm not smart enough to do this. Pessimistic negative attitude to life and a feeling of hopelessness about the future.
4. Perfectionism - Willingness to try things you know you can only complete perfectly and successfully. Unwilling to accept constructive criticism or help. Concern about what others will

think of you if you fail or don›t do well.

5. Angry, irritable, and unable to maintain relationships.

## Causes of Fear of Failure.

1. Family history: If you have any mental health disorders, such as phobias, anxiety, or depression, that run in your family, you are more likely to have these disorders.

2. Learned Behavior: You may have grown up in an environment where people taught you that failure is unacceptable or that anything less than perfect is a failure.

3. Underlying phobias: Sometimes phobias occur together. For example, a child with scolionophobia (fear of school) may also have atychiphobia. Or someone with mysophobia (fear of dirt and germs) may develop atychiphobia if they feel they are constantly not keeping clean.

4. Traumatic experiences: If you've suffered abuse or severe punishment as a result of failure, you may fear experiencing those

consequences again. Or you may feel guilty that your previous failures led to a horrific outcome, such as death or destruction.

5. Patterns learned from parents. Parents have a tremendous influence on their children in terms of fear of failure. Children whose parents are overprotective or place a high value on achievement and success can increase the likelihood that their child will develop a fear of failure.

6. Genetic and biological problems. Parents can influence fear phobia through their actions and communication, but they can also influence the condition through their biological makeup and genes, as fear has a genetic component. If a parent or other close relative has a phobia, the child is much more likely to have the same fear

7. Perfectionism: Someone with an intense and uncontrolled need for perfectionism might develop an associated fear of failure. When people are so intent on presenting themselves as perfect, any failure becomes unacceptable and greatly feared.

## Causes of Failure in Life.

*i.* Having Critical and Unsupportive Parents: Growing up routinely undermined and humiliated can carry these negative feelings into adulthood.

ii. Traumatic experience: For example, if you're interviewed and fail multiple times, you may never want to be interviewed again.

iii. Frequent procrastination. Avoidance of tasks or people related to a project or general goal.

v. Physical symptoms (fatigue, headache, indigestion, joint or muscle pain) that prevent you from working towards a goal.

vi. Being unprepared while taking an action can also impact the outcome of an action. For example, one may be failing in many business ventures because of not taking necessary preparations like doing enough research on the type of business and necessary actions to take before starting the business and doing a pro and cons analysis.

Rushing into business without necessary preparations to minimize the risks and maximize the opportunity could always lead to failure. One may think they are destined for failure and may fear ever starting something new for fear that it will always end up in failure just like the previous ventures.

vii. vi. Failure to involve God for divine guidance and direction: The steps of a righteous man are ordered by the Lord. Divine guidance is an essential ingredient for victory and success in life. (Proverbs 3:5-6, 21:31). Since God promises to guide us in all our ways, the first step as a believer is prayer, to seek divine guidance.

This is an essential part of the preparation. Never go blindly. Direction includes what, how, where, when, and with whom. If we lack this preparation even in normal day-to-day tasks, the likelihood of failure is higher since the timing, place, procedure, and partners are very crucial to the success of the venture we are set to undertake. Make sure you understand God's will before you act. The blessing and presence of God make all the difference.

vii. Demonic opposition

The devil is your adversary and will always stage attacks, and opposition to hamper your progress. Closed doors, uncommon failure, setbacks, stagnation, persistent misfortunes, and perennial defeats are some of the indicators of demonic activities. You need to step up prayers to neutralize the opposition.

You cannot be successful in life without exercising some measure of spiritual authority. ***"From the days of John the Baptist until now the kingdom of heaven has suffered violence, and the violent take it by force"*** (Matt.11:12 NIV). You must exert spiritual force to accelerate your success. Resist the devil and he will flee from you.

## How to deal with Fear of Failure.

1. Analyze all potential outcomes; fear of the unknown hinders many from taking new risks. Analyzing all potential outcomes of the decisions helps one to get ready for any eventuality.

2. Practice positive thinking: positive thinking helps in building

personal esteem and confidence to deal with self-sabotage. Every time a negative thought hinders progress one does great sabotage towards succeeding in their lives.

3. Analyze and prepare for the worst-case scenario: in most cases, the worst-case scenario may be genuinely intimidating but will help you prepare adequately.

4. Have an alternative plan just in case the first doesn't work so that it cautions your anxiety from failure.

5. Set small smart goals and plan how to achieve them. Those small gains will motivate you to move forward to bigger goals.

6. Resort to prayer for success and victory (Proverbs 21:31).

## Biblical Principles of Overcoming Fear of Failure.

Peter and his Companions.

***"One day as Jesus was standing by the Lake of Gennesaret, the people were crowding around him and listening to the word of God. He saw at the water's edge two boats, left there by the fishermen, who***

***were washing their nets. He got into one of the boats, the one belonging to Simon, and asked him to put out a little from shore. Then he sat down and taught the people from the boat.***

***When he had finished speaking, he said to Simon, "Put out into deep water, and let down the nets for a catch."***

***Simon answered, "Master, we've worked hard all night and haven't caught anything. But because you say so, I will let down the nets."***

***When they had done so, they caught such a large number of fish that their nets began to break. So they signaled their partners in the other boat to come and help them, and they came and filled both boats so full that they began to sink"*** Luke 5:1-6.

Principles of overcoming failure from this text.

1. Partnership with God is the foundation for true success (Luke 5:3). Jesus was about His father's business while Peter was about his fishing business. To effectively preach the Gospel to the pressing crowd, Jesus requested Peter for his boat to preach from, and he gave it up without a reservation. When Jesus fin-

ished preaching, He instructed Peter to let down the net for a catch. He managed to fish so much that his nets began to snap and the boat nearly sank.

2. You may experience the greatest Failure on the verge of your greatest Success (Luke5:2). After toiling for the whole night, Peter and his companions got nothing. In the morning, while they were desperate and washing their nets to head home, Jesus appeared in their situation. When Jesus appears in your situation, transforms your Worst into your Best.

3. Obedience is the key that unlocks your success (Luke 5:4-5). Jesus gave Peter simple but clear instructions; *"Launch into the deep and let down your net for a catch"*. Peter's success was tied to his obedience. Diligently obey the instructions God gave you to unlock your breakthroughs.

4. You can succeed where you failed before. The same Peter, same boat, same nets, and same lake but great success. The place of your greatest failure can become the platform for your greatest success. Be willing to try one more time.

5. Failure can position you to become a channel of God's blessings (Luke 5:6-7). When Peter caught so much fish that his net was breaking, he readily invited his companions and they too filled their boat with fish. Peter was not selfish and became the channel of God's blessing and success to others. The Failure he experienced humbled him.

NOTES

# Chapter 6

# OVERCOMING JOB-RELATED FEARS AND RETIREMENT ANXIETIES.

After the fall of man in the Garden of Eden, God cursed man and told him that henceforth he would eat of the sweat of his brow (Genesis 3:17-19). From then on work became the means by which people satisfy their needs. God is still merciful to man and blesses the work of his hands so that it prospers.

God gives rain in its season to water the earth so that it will bloom and provide food for mankind. Despite man's duty to work, God is still the ultimate Source and Sustainer of life. Man must acknowledge Him in all his endeavors. Work is therefore one of the means by which men meet their survival needs.

With high unemployment rates in Kenya and around the world, securing a job or employment is usually a nightmare. In Kenya, youth unemployment is currently over 65% while the minimum wage is $150. Despite the appropriate qualifications and experience, securing jobs is still a major challenge. A lack of income and high unemployment threatens the survival of many families. It is closely linked to high crime rates, poverty, poor living conditions, poor health, high-stress levels, drug addiction, and school drop-outs.

Statistically, there are few who secure decent and well-paying jobs, but even those who are underpaid do not wish to lose their jobs because it means everything to them. For many, working means more than just earning money; it also adds meaning and purpose to their lives. The Job makes them feel needed, productive, and useful and gives them a reason to get out of the house every day

Many Kenyans live in urban or suburban centers. Most live in rented houses and depend on their meager salaries for a living. These situations and demands explain why for many people their job is everything and they are thus afraid of losing it.

The thought of losing a job gives every employee sleepless nights. No one stomachs the news of retrenchment or layoffs. I recall the experience of a civil servant who was a member of my Church. He was working in Parastatal. Because of the crisis that the Parastatal was facing, the government laid off so many workers. Unfortunately, this brother was a victim. The decision came as a big shock to him. As a believer, he shared the matter with me and we prayed. The brother did not yield to fear but to faith. He purposed to report to his place of work as usual.

When the manager met him and asked what he was doing at work and yet he wasn't an employee. He appealed to him to be allowed to continue to come to work as usual on a voluntary basis since he had nothing else. Though it didn't make sense to the manager, he allowed it, assuming he'd give up within days.

Surprisingly, he reported to work for a whole month. At the end of the month, the manager was quite impressed and hired him back to his job. The most amazing thing is that he was promoted over time and rose in the ranks. Today he is General Manager of the Parastatal in Kenya. Learn to walk by faith instead of fear.

In my case, it was quite difficult to find a job after high school. I tarmacked for three and a half years (1972-1976). I applied unsuccessfully to many schools as an untrained teacher. I took part in Kenyan police and army recruitment exercises several times but was still unlucky. I ran out of options and resorted to casual labor. I worked on farms and drew water for people with donkeys. I kept praying and waiting for God and God miraculously gave me a breakthrough in 1976. A door opened and I joined civil service and where I worked in the Ministry of Finance.

Worked for 18 years until I voluntarily retired in 1994 the o join the full-time ministry. If you are faced with the challenge of finding employment, keep pressing in prayer and your breakthrough is guaranteed.

## How to overcome the Fear of an Interview.

1. Prepare carefully. Preparation is the foundation of a great and successful interview. It's an important step in managing your tension at the interview. To that end, you should make sure you have a strong, updated curriculum vitae with a professional layout. You should also dress for the highest job you want and be punctual for the interview.

**Never forget that sometimes things go better when they don't go your way. A greater and better opportunity may be just around the corner**

Prayer is paramount to enjoying God's favor, wisdom, courage, and strength

2. be open and ready for any outcome: It's paramount to step out by Faith expecting a Yes, but equally be ready for any eventuality. What if you don't get this job, will the world end? BIG NO! Will your life be worth less? BIG NO!

You are desperate financially and you surely need this job. If you don't get it, it will be painful, financially difficult, and certainly disappointing, but it won't be the end of you. You are strong. Never forget that sometimes things go better when they don't go your way. A greater and better opportunity may be just around the corner

## Handling Promotion Anxieties.

The promotion comes with qualifications and job experience. As people advance in their careers, they acquire the necessary skills and experience with the aim of getting promotion in terms of rank and emoluments. However, promotion is not automatic.

It's frustrating to stay in the same status when your promotion is overdue. It is even more tormenting when your juniors are in your place due to corruption and nepotism. As a Christian believer, this call for Prayers. True promotion in life comes from the Lord (Psalm 75:7-8).

When I worked at the Treasury Department, I seriously awaited my promotion after years of service. Unfortunately, my colleagues were promoted while I was on leave. As I resumed my work, I seriously took time to pray about the matter.

It was truly a devastating ordeal, but I chose to seek divine intervention. Miraculously, I was called in for an interview and almost immediately got my promotion. I glorify God because He controls the day of our Promotion. Work and promotion-related challenges can and should be overcome by prayers. Don't give in to fear but Stand out by Faith.

## How to deal with Retirement Anxieties

While retirement can be a reward for years of hard work, it can also cause stress, fear, and depression. However with the right preparations you find a new purpose, and flourish in your retirement.

## How to prepare for Retirement.

- Start investing your income early to earn the kind of income you need to cover your expenses in retirement.

- Take full benefit of Social Security and employer pensions. Whenever possible, increase your pension contributions up to the maximum allowed;

- Reduce your debts. Consider speeding up your mortgage payments so the loan is paid off before you retire. Limiting new debts and reducing existing debt will minimize the amount of retirement income that will be spent on payments of debts

- Calculate your projected retirement income. Estimate your projected income from sources such as Social Security and employer pensions, savings, and investments.

- Estimate your retirement expenses. Some expenses, such like Health care, may be higher later in life, while others, like commuting or clothing costs, among others, may decline.

## Guidelines to help you cope with Retirement Challenges.

1. Embrace change: Although an inevitable part of life, coping with change is never easy. But just as you transitioned from childhood into adulthood, accept and adjust to the transition from work to retirement.
2. Change your attitude. Approach retirement as a journey rather than a destination. Don't be rigid. Be flexible and review your decisions whenever necessary. Focusing on what you're gaining, rather than the things you're losing in retirement.
3. Develop resilience. The more resilient you are, the better you can handle challenges like retirement.
4. Accept the things that you cannot change. Struggling with events that you have no control over is exhausting and useless. Whatever the circumstances of your retirement is, accept them and refocus your effort on working on the things you have control over.
5. Redefine your identity. Many of us define ourselves by what we do for a living. After retirement, you can find new ways to

define yourself through non-work activities and relationships. Where you used to be an accountant, a teacher, a policeman, etc. you are now a mentor, grandparent, author, or artist among others.

6. Set yourself new goals in life. You may have already achieved many of your career goals in life, but it's important to keep setting yourself new goals to achieve. Having goals can energize you, give you purpose, and help redefine your identity. Set goals that challenge and inspire you to move forward in life.
7. Seek social support. You don't have to face the challenges of retirement planning alone. Many other people are going through the same difficulties. Reaching out and sharing the burden can help reduce your stress and strengthen your coping skills.
8. Reinforce your social network. Staying socially connected can have a huge impact on your mental health and happiness. You're never too old to make new, rewarding friendships.

NOTES

## Chapter 7

# OVERCOMING THE FEAR THAT PRECEDES A CALL INTO MINISTRY.

From the creation account in Genesis 1:26-27, we learn that God created man in His image, after His likeness. ***"Then God said, "Let Us make man in Our image, according to Our likeness; let them have dominion over the fish of the sea, over the birds of the air, and the cattle, over all the earth and over every creeping thing that creeps on the earth." So God created man in His own image; in the image of God He created him; male and female He created them"***

The word Image of God comes from the Latin word ***'Imago dei'***. It means similarity, resemblance, or likeness. Man possesses divine moral, spiritual, and intellectual attributes.

God created man to duplicate Himself. That's why He created him in his own image, after His own likeness. His original plan was that man should be like himself to represent him properly on earth. Man was to be a reflection of the glory, nature, and character of God to the rest of creation. He is God's representative and agent on earth.

To carry out His commission on earth, God always seeks, chooses, and calls a man or woman to work through. Examination of God's called servants reveals a challenge they all grumbled about; Fear. I will deal primarily with the two types of fear that precede a call to service and how to overcome them.

## 1. Fear of Incompetence.

All the men and women God called in the Bible were ordinary, inexperienced, and unqualified from the human perspective. Their immediate response to the great call of God was fear. They felt inadequate and incompetent to carry out the mandate given to them. They triumphed over their fears as they rose from their perception to God's perception of them.

According to the Bible, we are not disqualified by our natural attributes. We are qualified by the call of God. Many other heroes of Scripture had obvious limitations—for example, Moses stammered, had a criminal history, and was eighty years old when God called him to action. What qualified him in God's eyes was, 'I created you, I called you and I am with you.

What is Perception?

Your perception is your assessment of who you are (your identity) and what you are capable of. But is it God's perception of you? God is calling us to renew our perception, so we can do God's work wholeheartedly and without fear.

**According to the Bible, we are not disqualified by our natural attributes. We are qualified by the call of God. Many other heroes of Scripture had obvious limitations—for example, Moses stammered, had a criminal history, and was eighty years old when God called him to action. What qualified him in God's eyes was, 'I created you, I called you and I am with you.**

If God has given you a problem to solve, a call to serve, people to love, or ministry to accomplish, know this: He sees you as fully equipped for that role! You are not alone. You are empowered with the Holy Spirit. God is with you. God calls us to a life dependent on him.

The Holy Spirit is our Helper, teacher, and Counselor and helps us to do His work more efficiently. Acts 1:8 after the resurrection, before the ascension, Jesus told his disciples to wait and not leave Jerusalem until they receive power.

You have God's affirmation! Whatever your challenges in terms of physical attributes, position, or experience, don't let them affect your perception. See your weaknesses as opportunities for the manifestation of God's power. ***"But he said to me, My grace is sufficient for you, for my power is made perfect in weakness. "Therefore I will boast all the more gladly about my weaknesses, so that Christ's power may rest on me"*** (2 Corinthians 12:9 NIV.). See your limitations as an advantage; because God will be glorified through them.

Don't measure yourself against the task, opportunity, or other people and decide you are lacking. God sees you as a Hero. Press on to the mark of your higher calling.

## 2. Fear of Inadequacy.

Several of God's servants wrestle with the fear of inadequacy. Fear of inadequacy can cause God's servants to question their ability to serve effectively.

They feel unable to meet the needs of their family and ministry. The sense of inadequacy should evoke a sense of dependence on God rather than fear. If left unchecked, fear will create further challenges and become a major factor pushing you out of ministry. Face your fear with the Scriptures. Joshua was commanded not to be afraid (Joshua 1:9), we must equally fight the fear within us with the sword of His Word. God's providence is undeniable.

Build your trust in God by spending time reading the Bible and absorbing the Word of God. The more you read about God's power, faithfulness, and love, the more assured you will be in the Lord's calling and placement. As your faith grows, God will endow you with divine resources to carry out His commission.

NOTES

# Chapter 8

# OVERCOMING FEAR OF NOT GETTING MARRIED OR BEING DIVORCED

## Institution of Marriage

Marriage was instituted by God in the Garden of Eden (Genesis 2:20-25). A Christian marriage is a marriage that has been instituted by and operates according to Biblical principles.

A Christian marriage is a union and lifetime commitment between a man and a woman (Genesis 2:24, Mathew 19; 4-5).

As one grows older and matures, one becomes more distant from one's parents and the environment in which one was born and raised. One begins to seek direction in life and pursue his or her own goals in life. During this stage, you no longer need your parents, but a suitable partner with whom you can spend your life; a spouse with whom life goals are closely connected.

So the first major life event after independence is marriage, However, for some, marriage is not easy. They experience many difficulties, obstacles, and resistance. Over time, they start to feel late, and the fear of not getting married creeps in. If you are in this situation, these tips will help you overcome your fear.

## How to cope with the Fear of not getting Married.

1. Don't despair- Desperation is a very unattractive attitude. It is not a crime to be unmarried at 30 or above. No law says you must be married at a fixed age. Therefore, don't judge yourself too harshly. Hope is the anchor of the soul (Hebrews 12:0 If You walk by faith and hope in God, your expectation of one day being married will never be disappointed.

2. Free yourself. ***"You have been trapped by what you said, ensnared by the words of your mouth"*** (Proverbs 6; 2). You can be trapped and be ensnared by the words of your mouth. If at any point you have vowed never to marry out of frustration, these words are still active and will fight your efforts to get married. You have to free yourself first.

***"Allow no sleep to your eyes, nor slumber to your eyelids. Free yourself, like a gazelle from the hand of the hunter, like a bird from the snare of the fowler"*** (Proverbs 6:4-5).

3. Don't compromise. Resolve not to defile yourselves (Daniel 1:8). Maintain the purity and sanctity of your body. Righteousness will exalt you.

4. Don't subscribe to the subtle and damaging contemporary belief of the "independent Woman" philosophy. It has kept so many women from getting married. It causes some women to go into relationships with a boastful and competitive attitude that turns men off (and vice-versa).

5. Some women have chosen to remain single. There is no crime in that. But there is no such thing as an independent woman or man. It›s a myth because we›re all designed to connect. A woman needs a man and a man needs a woman.

6. Be patient. There is a time for everything, and a season for every activity under the heavens (Ecclesiastes 3:1,). In due time, God

will make everything beautiful. Wait patiently for the Lord. He will draw you to the right person at the right time

## How to cope with the Fear of Divorce.

Solid marriages are the foundation of a vibrant church, community, nation, and the world. For this reason, we must recognize marriages are a strategic target of Satan.

In Matthew 19:1-12, the Pharisees came to Jesus and asked a subtle question, «Is it lawful for a man to divorce his wife for any and every reason?" Jesus was preaching on the territory at that point of Herod Antipas. Herod had ordered the imprisonment and execution of John the Baptist for preaching so strongly against his sinful marriage to Herodias, his Brother Philip's wife.

***'"Haven't you read," he replied, "that at the beginning the Creator 'made them male and female,' and said, 'For this reason, a man will leave his father and mother and be united to his wife, and the two will become one flesh? So they are no longer two, but one flesh. Therefore what God has joined together, let no one separate. "Why then," they***

***asked, "did Moses command that a man give his wife a certificate of divorce and send her away?"***

***Jesus replied, "Moses permitted you to divorce your wives because your hearts were hard. But it was not this way from the beginning. I tell you that anyone who divorces his wife, except for sexual immorality, and marries another woman commits adultery." (Matthew*** 19:4-6).

Jesus' answer shows that God hates divorce. Divorce is rooted in a person's hardness of heart. It is the main cause of divorce. The hardness of the heart is simply not yielding to God and His commandments. It is habitual rebellion and opposition to God. Jesus says the permission for Moses

It is of paramount importance to be vigilant and protect your marriage from any aggression from the enemy. Fully subscribe to and work upon the biblical principle of marriage. Don't give the devil a hold to torment you for fear of being abandoned or divorced. If the devil fails to stop you from getting married, he will try to prevent you from enjoying it.

I remember a lady who used to come to me asking for prayers because she was very afraid that her husband would put her away. But even after praying several times, she did not overcome her fear. Finally, what she feared happened. Her husband acquired American citizenship and traveled to the USA.

She had no option but t to be left behind because the children were still young and in school. For two years she was left behind, but after persistent prayers, God intervened and way for her to join her husband in the United States. Although her case did not end in divorce, the devil tormented her for many years and stole her peace and joy in marriage through fear.

. ***"Do not be anxious about anything, but in every situation, by prayer and petition, with thanksgiving, present your requests to God. And the peace of God, which transcends all understanding, will guard your hearts and your minds in Christ Jesus"*** (Philippians 4:6)

NOTES

# Chapter 9

## OVERCOMING FEAR OF DEATH.

Fear of death also known as Thanatophobia is a form of anxiety characterized by a fear of one's death or the process of dying. It is commonly referred to as death anxiety. It derives from the Greek words ***"Thanatos"*** which refers to death and ***"Phobia"*** which means fear.

Thanatophobia is different from **necrophobia,** which is a general fear of dead or dying things, or things associated with death.

Having some death anxiety is an entirely normal part of the human condition. However, for some people, thinking about their death or the process of dying can lead to extreme anxiety and fear.

A person can feel extreme anxiety and fear considering that death is inevitable. You may also experience fear of separation, fear of coping with a loss and worry about leaving loved ones behind. When such fears persist and interfere with daily life and activities, it is known as thanatophobia. In extreme cases, these feelings can prevent people from going about their daily activities or even leaving their homes. Your fears focus on things that could lead to death, such as contamination or dangerous objects and people.

## The Biblical view of Death.

When God created man, he placed him in the Garden of Eden. He allowed him to eat all the fruit in the garden except the tree that stood in the middle of the garden; the tree of the knowledge of good and evil.

The result of disobedience was death (Genesis 2:16-17). The devil deceived them cunningly and through sin, death came to all People (Genesis 3:1-8). ***"Therefore, just as through one man sin entered the world, and death through sin, and thus death spread to all men because all sinned"*** (Romans 5:12).

Originally, people lived more than nine hundred years (Genesis 5:1-25), but because of the increase in wickedness, God reduced their years to one hundred and twenty years ***"And the Lord said, "My Spirit shall not strive with man forever, for he is indeed flesh; yet his days shall be one hundred and twenty years."*** (Genesis 6; 3)

Over time, due to the inclination of man toward evil, life span has reduced to 70 or 80 years ( Psalm 90:10, ***" The years of our life are seventy, or even by reason of strength eighty; yet their span is but toil and trouble; they are soon gone, and we fly away".***

In a Biblical context, death essentially means separation. There are three categories of death:

a) Physical death: This is the separation of the body and the spirit. Physical death is a transition from this life to eternity.

b) Spiritual death: Separation between God and man. God is essentially the source and sustainer of human life. When one's relationship with God is broken, he is disconnected from their source of life, thus dead spiritually even though physically he may be alive.

c) Eternal death: This is eternal separation from God. ***"Then Death and Hades were thrown into the lake of fire. This is the second death, the lake of fire. And if anyone's name was not found written in the book of life, he was thrown into the lake of fire"*** (Rev. 21:14-15)

Hebrews 2:15 **says, "And free those who all their lives were held in slavery by their fear of death."**(NIV).

Jesus was revealed to deliver all who are enslaved by fear of death.

## How to overcome the Fear of Death.

1. Accept the reality of death. "And as it is appointed for men to die once, but after this the judgment," (Hebrews 10:27). God Has appointed men to die. Death is a reality for everybody.

2. Reject premature death. Although death is a reality for everyone, God also numbered our days. He plans to give us a full life span. ***"…I will give you a full life span"*** (Exodus 23:26 NIV) Declare like David, ***"I shall not die, but live,***

3. ***And declare the works of the Lord"*** (Psalm 118:17). Refuse to die before you fulfill your assignment on Earth.

4. Avoid Sin. Physical death came as a result of sin, ***"Therefore, just as sin came into the world through one man, and death through sin, and so death spread to all men because***

***all sinned"*** (Romans 5:12). The wages of sin is death, ***"For the wages of sin is death, but the free gift of God is eternal life in Christ Jesus our Lord"*** (Romans 6:23). The power of death (sting) is sin, to overcome death, overcome sin, ***"Death is swallowed up in victory." O death, where is your victory? O death, where is your sting?" The sting of death is sin, and the power of sin is the law"*** (1 Corinthians 15:54-56). Sin shortens lifespan (Genesis 6:3).

5. Accept Jesus as your Lord and Savior. Jesus will set you free from the power of sin, give you eternal life and resurrect your body on the day of resurrection (1Corinthians 15:50-58).

6. Understand Physical death is a transition into eternity. The Earth is a temporary resident of Man. We are all on our journey to our eternal Home. Flesh and blood cannot inherit the kingdom of God, ***"I tell you this, brothers: flesh and blood cannot inherit the kingdom of God, nor does the perishable inherit the imperishable"*** (1 cor. 15:50). To be absent in the body is to be present with the Lord.

7. Rebuke and cast out the Spirit of fear of death out of your life. You have been given authority over all evil spirits, death included (Luke (:11).

Unfortunately, I remember a case I experienced a few years ago. It happened during my routine church visits. In this Sunday service, I taught the topic of fear and how to overcome it. I highlighted different types of fear people experience.

After preaching, I fellowshipped with various people before they dispersed. One of them was I a gentleman in his early 30s. During our discourse, he confirmed that the sermon was indeed relevant but told me that I did not mention his fear. I asked about his fear and without hesitation said that he was afraid of dying young (early death). I prayed and encouraged him to face and overcome that fear.

After about five years, I returned to minister in that church. After ministration, I inquired about the whereabouts of this young man since he was missing from the Sunday service.

To my greatest shock, I was informed he passed away. Regrettably, his wife died two years after his death. You must confront and overcome the fear of death and nagging thoughts of suicide in Jesus' name.

NOTES

# Chapter 10

## BIBLICAL PRINCIPLES FOR OVERCOMING FEAR.

### 1. Build a Positive Self-Image.

Essentially, fear stems from a negative self-Image. Self-image is one's personal view, concept, or Perception. It is the mental picture that we have of ourselves. Self-image is internal programming or a dictionary that defines who you are.

Self-image (how you see yourself) determines your self-esteem and self-confidence, which consequently determines how you feel, behave, and act.

### Biblical examples.

Adam and Eve: When Adam sinned, he expressed fear for the first time in human history (Genesis 3:7-10). Why were they afraid? After eating the forbidden fruit, Genesis 3:7 clearly states that their eyes were opened and they saw themselves naked. For the first time, the man saw himself negatively and reacted with fear.

We can deduce from this text that the primary and greatest damaging effect of sin was on self-image. Fear was the result of how they saw themselves.

The ten spies: Moses sent twelve Heads of Tribes of Israel to spy on the land of Canaan. After forty days, they returned to the camp and brought their feedback (Numbers 13:1-33). Numbers 13:33 records, "…***We seemed like grasshoppers in our own eyes, and we looked the same to them.***"

Ten spies brought a bad and intimidating report. They saw themselves as a grasshopper and their negative self-image amplified their challenges and triggered panic.

Your self-image determines how you see, interpret and react to the realities of life. Indicators of negative self-image include low self-esteem (value), self-rejection, self-belittling, low self-esteem, and fear.

The first step to overcoming fear is cultivating and developing a positive self-image. A positive self-image leads to high self-esteem, high self-confidence, outrageous boldness, and courage. Self-image is important because how we think about ourselves affects how we interact with others and the world around us. A positive self-image can increase our physical, mental, social, emotional, and spiritual well-being. On the other hand, a negative self-image can reduce our satisfaction and performance in these areas.

We can learn to develop a healthier and more accurate view of ourselves and thus challenge the distortions. Self-image changes throughout life. A healthy self-image starts with learning to accept and love ourselves.

## How to develop a Healthy/Positive self –Image.

a) Take stock of your self-image. You can only start where you are. Take your time to get your bearings

b) Make a list of your positive qualities. A negative self-Image focuses more on your weakness. Refocus your attention on your strengths.

c) Ask important people in your life to describe your positive qualities.

d) Set personal goals that are reasonable and achievable.

e) Counteract distorted thoughts.

f) Identify and explore the impact of negative childhood labels. Begin to undo them with positive labels that better define you.

g) Refrain from comparing yourself to others.

h) Develop your strengths.

i) Learn to love yourself.

j) Give positive affirmations to others.

k) Remember that you are unique.

l) Remember how far you've come.

## 2. Build positive Thoughts.

Fear springs from our own minds and imagination. That's why psychologists like to say that fear represents fantasized experiences that appear real. Under ordinary circumstances, anxiety can be triggered by specific situations and life-threatening circumstances that fuel a spectrum of anxiety.

However, there is another spectrum of fear that comes from within, and the culprit is often our negative thoughts and low self-esteem. Most likely, it is this very fear that is preventing you from living the highly successful, lush, and joyful life you long for.

The Law of Replacement dictates that you cannot replace something with nothing – you have to replace it with something else. So if you find yourself experiencing a negative, fear-inducing thought, replace it with a positive thought instead.

To dominate your mind with positive thoughts, feed it positive information. The Bible is the greatest source of positive divine thoughts and plans for man. Feed your spirit with the Word of God.

***"Finally, brothers and sisters, whatever is true, whatever is noble, whatever is right, whatever is pure, whatever is lovely, whatever is admirable—if anything is excellent or praiseworthy—think about such things"(*** Philippians 4:7).

### Build your Faith.

The opposite of Fear is Faith. The two are mutually exclusive. By focusing on building and increasing your Faith, Fear inadvertently diminish. You can only replace fear with Faith

Now take that negative statement and write an empowering positive statement that is the opposite of your limiting beliefs. Apostle Paul teaches that Faith comes by hearing the of God (Romans10:17).

Take that very first step in the positive direction. Yes, the first step is often the hardest. Remember to take one step at a time. Apostle James says that Faith without action is dead (James 2:14-20).

When the going gets tough, be patient with yourself and the process you're going through and eventually you will make progress.

### 5. Chose Positive Relationships.

We were created and wired for the relationship. Relationships can bring us great joy or deep distress. The most important thing in life is your relationships. Foremost, your relationship with God, and then, your relationships with other people. We are made to go through life together with others.

Positive means **a** relationship between people who accept, appreciate, respect, encourage and support each other emotionally, spiritually, and physically (practically). Surround yourself with people who affirm and provoke you to be optimistic through their words, actions and accomplishments.

***"The righteous choose their friends carefully, but the way of the wicked leads them astray"*** (Proverbs 12:26 NIV).

### 6. Speak the Word of God in your Situation:

What we believe in or fear is first demonstrated in our irrational thoughts and finally in our speech and conduct. Proverbs 18:21 enlightens us that life and death are in the power of the tongue. When the devil tempted Jesus, He overcame Him by quoting the Holy Scriptures (Matt. 4:-11).

We are called upon to put on the full armor of God and the word of God is our Sword. The word of God in your mouth is a weapon of mass destruction for the kingdom of Satan. As you proclaim the word, you will not only cast out fear but you will transform your situations.

### 7. Rebuke the Spirit of Fear.

***"For God has not given us a spirit of fear, but of power and of love and of a sound mind"*** (2 Timothy 1:7).

Apostle Paul in his address to his son in Faith Timothy acknowledges Fear as a spirit.

Other than being an emotion, we must be aware of the spiritual aspect of fear. Paralyzing fear is beyond emotions. In such situations, Exercise your God-given authority to rebuke and cast out Fear out of your life in Jesus' Name.

NOTES

# CONCLUSION.

## PRAYER.

If you are not born again, please pray this prayer aloud to accept Jesus and register your name in the Book of Life.

***Dear Lord Jesus Christ, I believe with all my heart that you died on the cross for my sin. I confess that Jesus is my Lord and Savior. Forgive me my sins and write my name in the Lamb's book of life. Give me your Holy Spirit to help me on this journey of salvation. In the name of Jesus, I pray.***

***Amen***

Now that you are born again by accepting Jesus as Lord and Savior, please strive to grow in Him by joining a Christ-centered fellowship of brothers (church) and through daily prayer and Bible reading. For believers, fix your eyes on Jesus, the author, and finisher of your faith

## Prayer to overcome the Spirit of Fear.

My Father in heaven, I thank you for creating me in your image and likeness. You have given me the Spirit of power, Love, and sound mind not the Spirit of Fear.

In the Name of Jesus, I command the spirit of fear to come out of my life now in Jesus' Name.

The Fear of: Losing family inheritance, failure, death, not getting married, divorce, fear of heights, fear of large bodies of water, fear of darkness, fear of open space, fear of certain insects, fear of animals, and fear of any other fear you are experiencing, Come out of life.

I command you to lose my emotions and mind. I close every door that I opened to the enemy out of fear. I put to an end every torment of the enemy now.

I invite you Holy Spirit of God to deliver and empower me now in Jesus' Name. I will live by Faith from now on. I receive my freedom from every torment of fear.

In Jesus' name, I pray.

Amen.

NOTES

## ABOUT THE AUTHOR

PRESBYTER DR. JAMES WAWERU MWAURA was born on February 12, 1948, in the Passenga Scheme in Nyandarua County. He is the firstborn of JOSEPH MWAURA and REBBECCA WANJIRU. He is married to PST MARY WAWERU and together they have been blessed with 12 children and over 41 grandchildren.

He attended elementary school from 1958 to 1966, when he took his CPE final exam. He entered high school in 1969 and passed his fourth-grade EACE exam in 1972. He had various occupations and business ventures until 1975. In 1976 he entered the civil service, where he worked in the Ministry of Treasury; Finance department. He served faithfully for 18 years until he retired in 1994 to join the full-time ministry.

On February 16, 1974, he accepted the Lord Jesus Christ as his Savior and joined the Full Gospel Church. In 1978 he joined the CHRIST CO-WORKERS FELLOWSHIP (CHRISCO) right at the inception and onset in Kenya. He was nurtured, trained, and raised by the founders: Apostle Harry Das and Minister C. Das. He became a committed member, worker, and leader.

He has served in various capacities including deacon: Elder, Pastor, National Head of Ushers, National Treasurer, Presbyter, Apostolic Representative, and National Chairman Chrisco Kenya. He has been a committed member and loyal leader of the Chrisco Fellowship over the last 45 years. In 2016 he received an Honorary Doctorate in Theology from Cambridge Theological Seminary for exemplary service and leadership.

## REFRENCES

**Claims under the Inheritance (Provision for Family and Dependents) Act 1975**

**Published on 12 December 2019**

**Blood & Money: Why Families Fight Over Inheritance BY P. MARK ACCETTURA, J.D.**

NOTES

www.ingramcontent.com/pod-product-compliance
Lightning Source LLC
LaVergne TN
LVHW010112170826
845678LV00012B/2358

* 9 7 9 8 8 3 8 1 5 5 0 5 4 *